W9-AYO-550

Date: 10/6/15

J 796.33264 TAM
Temple, Ramey.
Tampa Bay Buccaneers /

Tampa Bay Buccaneers

BY RAMEY TEMPLE

AV² provides enriched content that supplements and complements this book. Weigl's AV² books strive to create inspired learning and engage young minds in a total learning experience.

Your AV² Media Enhanced books come alive with...

Audio
Listen to sections of the book read aloud.

Key Words
Study vocabulary, and complete a matching word activity.

Video
Watch informative video clips.

Quizzes
Test your knowledge.

Go to **www.av2books.com**, and enter this book's unique code.

BOOK CODE

F 8 8 7 7 6 4

Embedded Weblinks
Gain additional information for research.

Slide Show
View images and captions, and prepare a presentation.

AV² by Weigl brings you media enhanced books that support active learning.

Try This!
Complete activities and hands-on experiments.

... and much, much more!

Published by AV² by Weigl
350 5ᵗʰ Avenue, 59ᵗʰ Floor
New York, NY 10118
Websites: www.av2books.com   www.weigl.com

Library of Congress Control Number: 2014930839

ISBN 978-1-4896-0898-7 (hardcover)
ISBN 978-1-4896-0900-7 (single-user eBook)
ISBN 978-1-4896-0901-4 (multi-user eBook)

Printed in the United States of America in North Mankato, Minnesota
1 2 3 4 5 6 7 8 9 0 18 17 16 15 14

042014
WEP150314

Project Coordinator Aaron Carr
Art Director Terry Paulhus

Photo Credits
Every reasonable effort has been made to trace ownership and to obtain permission to reprint copyright material. The publishers would be pleased to have any errors or omissions brought to their attention so that they may be corrected in subsequent printings.

Weigl acknowledges Getty Images as its primary image supplier for this title.

Tampa Bay Buccaneers

CONTENTS

Introduction

The Tampa Bay Buccaneers earned a reputation as lovable losers after dropping their first 26 games, a National Football League (NFL) record. Just two years after ending their losing streak, the **expansion team** with the bright orange uniforms found themselves facing the Los Angeles Rams with a trip to the **Super Bowl** at stake.

After losing to the Rams at a rain-soaked Tampa Stadium, the Bucs geared up for another record-setting streak. Beginning in 1983, they lost 10 games or more in 12 straight seasons. During that span of losing, they famously traded future Pro Football **Hall of Famer** Steve Young to the San Francisco 49ers.

The Buccaneers are one of only three teams to win their lone Super Bowl game. The New York Jets and New Orleans Saints are the other two.

The franchise changed entirely when coach Tony Dungy took over in 1995. The Bucs became winners, finishing **.500** or better in 11 of the next 16 seasons. Their greatest moment came under coach Jon Gruden as a dynamic defense crushed the Oakland Raiders in Super Bowl XXXVII.

Doug Martin has been a running back for the Buccaneers since 2012.

Stadium Raymond James Stadium

Division National Football Conference (NFC) South

Head coach Lovie Smith

Location Tampa, Florida

Super Bowl titles 2002

Nicknames The Bucs

10
Playoff Appearances

1
Super Bowl Championship

3
NFC Championships

History

BRRRRR!

Until they won a 2002 game in frigid Chicago, the warm-weather Buccaneers lost 20 straight games in which the temperature at kickoff was below 40 °Fahrenheit (4 °Celsius).

Warren Sapp was one of only three players to be named to the All-Decade Team in both the 1990s and 2000s by the Pro Football Hall of Fame voters.

n 1976, the Tampa Bay Buccaneers joined the Seattle Seahawks as the first two expansion teams after the American Football League-NFL **merger**. The Bucs began play in the tough American Football Conference (AFC) West. After suffering through a 26-game losing streak, they shocked the sports world by starting the 1979 season with a 5–0 win-loss record. A crushing defense led by Lee Roy Selmon helped the Bucs finish the season 10–6, on their way to their first division title.

The Bucs reached the **playoffs** for the third time in four years in 1982, but as quickly as they had risen, they began to fall. 1983 marked the first of 14 straight losing seasons. This streak came to an end in 1997, a year after coach Tony Dungy was hired.

The Bucs had grown into a yearly contender by the time coach Gruden took over a record-setting defense in 2002. **Pro Bowler** Derrick Brooks earned Defensive Player of the Year honors in leading the Bucs to a 12–4 record. Defense was the key as the Bucs stormed through the playoffs, capturing their lone Super Bowl championship against the Oakland Raiders by a score of 48-21.

Derrick Brooks was elected to the Pro Bowl 11 times, which tied him for the second most appearances by a linebacker in NFL history.

The Stadium

Raymond James Stadium holds 65,857 fans.

The Bucs began play at Tampa Stadium, also known as "The Big Sombrero," in 1976. The stadium opened in 1967 and was demolished 32 years later in 1999. The demolition followed the opening of Raymond James Stadium, which is sometimes referred to as "The New Sombrero."

Bucs fans welcome the cannon fire from Raymond James Stadium as the noise signals another Bucs score.

Construction on the new stadium began shortly after Malcolm Glazer purchased the team. The Chicago Bears came to town to face the Bucs in the first game at Raymond James Stadium on September 20, 1998, a 27-15 Bucs victory. The stadium has also played host to two Super Bowls, first in 2001, and again in 2009.

An incredible feature of the Raymond James Stadium, or "Ray Jay," is the 103-foot (31-meter) replica pirate ship. The ship sits harbored in Buccaneer Cove, just in front of a fantastical fishing village. A remote-controlled, animated parrot sits on the stern, or rear, of the ship throughout the game, talking to fans as they pass.

The Cuban sandwich at the Crow's Nest is both messy and delicious, overflowing with pork, ham, cheese, and salami.

Where They Play

CANADA

Washington **30**

Oregon

Montana

North Dakota

Lake Superior

Minnesota

Wisconsin **23**

22

Idaho

Iowa

24

29

Nevada

Utah

Wyoming

South Dakota

Nebraska

13

Illinois

14

15

California

Colorado

Kansas

Missouri

31

UNITED STATES

16

Arizona

New Mexico

Oklahoma

Arkansas

32

Pacific Ocean

Texas

17

27 Mississippi

Louisiana

12

MEXICO

Gulf of Mexico

Alaska

0   500 Miles
0   500 km

Hawai'i

0   100 Miles
0   100 km

AMERICAN FOOTBALL CONFERENCE

EAST		NORTH		SOUTH		WEST	
1	Gillette Stadium	5	FirstEnergy Stadium	9	EverBank Field	13	Arrowhead Stadium
2	MetLife Stadium	6	Heinz Field	10	LP Field	14	Sports Authority Field at Mile High
3	Ralph Wilson Stadium	7	M&T Bank Stadium	11	Lucas Oil Stadium	15	O.co Coliseum
4	Sun Life Stadium	8	Paul Brown Stadium	12	NRG Stadium	16	Qualcomm Stadium

RAYMOND JAMES STADIUM

Location
4201 North Dale Mabry Highway
Tampa, Florida

Broke ground
October 15, 1996

Completed
September 20, 1998

Surface
Tifway 419 bermudagrass

Features
- a 43-ton (39-metric ton) steel-and-concrete replica of a pirate ship is permanently harbored in Buccaneer Cove

Map Labels

Lake Michigan
Lake Huron
Lake Ontario
Lake Erie

New Hampshire
Maine
Vermont
New York
Massachusetts — 1
Rhode Island
Michigan — 21
3
2
Connecticut
19
20
Pennsylvania
11
New Jersey
18
Ohio
5
6
Delaware
8
Maryland
Indiana
West Virginia
7
Kentucky
Virginia
10
North Carolina
Tennessee
25
South Carolina
Georgia — 26
Alabama
Atlantic Ocean
9
Florida
28
4

0 — 250 Miles
0 — 250 Kilometers

LEGEND
- American Football Conference
- National Football Conference
- ☆ Raymond James Stadium

NATIONAL FOOTBALL CONFERENCE

EAST	NORTH	SOUTH	WEST
17 AT&T Stadium	21 Ford Field	25 Bank of America Stadium	29 Levi's Stadium
18 FedExField	22 Lambeau Field	26 Georgia Dome	30 CenturyLink Field
19 Lincoln Financial Field	23 Mall of America Field	27 Mercedes-Benz Superdome	31 Edward Jones Dome
20 MetLife Stadium	24 Soldier Field	☆28 Raymond James Stadium	32 University of Phoenix Stadium

The Uniforms

COLOR CHANGE

In 1976, the Bucs first picked **RED, GREEN, ORANGE, & WHITE** as their team colors. However, the green looked too much like the **MIAMI DOLPHINS'** color, and was replaced with another shade of orange.

 Lavonte David has played in all 32 games during his two seasons in Tampa Bay, averaging 8.84 tackles per game.

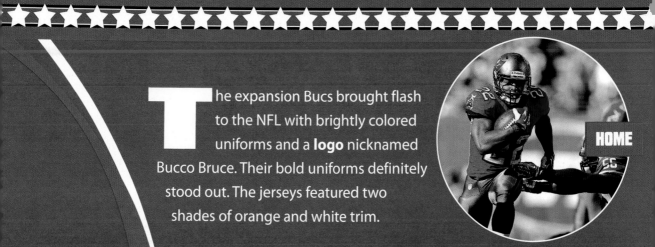

The expansion Bucs brought flash to the NFL with brightly colored uniforms and a **logo** nicknamed Bucco Bruce. Their bold uniforms definitely stood out. The jerseys featured two shades of orange and white trim.

HOME

Bucco Bruce was replaced by a sword and a battle flag in 1997 as the Bucs went through a complete redesign of their logo, uniforms, and color scheme. A pirate ship logo was added to the sleeves of the jersey, and team colors changed to red, pewter, black, and a dash of orange. The Bucs have since added a black **alternate jersey** to their home game rotation.

AWAY

NFL team captains wear a "C" on their jerseys so they are easy to identify as leaders.

The Helmets

HANDS OFF!

In 2003, the Oakland Raiders sued the Buccaneers, claiming Tampa Bay was using a version of the Raiders' pirate logo. The lawsuit was later thrown out.

When the Bucs released their new uniform look in March 2014, the helmet's pirate logo had increased in size.

The first Bucs helmets were white, with orange and red stripes. The helmets also had a Buccaneer logo on the side, which is no longer in use. The red and orange logo was an image of a pirate nicknamed Bruce the Buccaneer, or "Bucco Bruce." The artist who designed Bucco Bruce was faced with the challenge of creating a pirate logo that looked different from the Oakland Raiders' pirate. Bruce was a lighthearted pirate, and although he was holding a knife in his mouth, he appeared to be winking. A local sports writer joked that Bruce was a pirate who struck fear into no one.

In 1996, when the Bucs changed their image, the winking pirate was replaced with a red flag displaying a white pirate skull with two crossed swords and a football. The helmet went from white to pewter, with light orange pinstripes that linked to the former colors.

Football is a very physical sport. Helmets, as well as leg and shoulder pads, are required to keep players safe.

The Coaches

2 The number of Bucs coaches, Tony Dungy and Jon Gruden, who left Tampa Bay with a winning record.

⅃ Lovie Smith's coaching career began at Big Sandy High School in 1980. He became the head coach of the Tampa Bay Buccaneers 34 years later.

John McKay coached the Bucs during their first eight seasons. McKay took a beating from the media when the team started with a 26-game losing streak. Despite the criticism, McKay coached the Bucs in 133 games, making him the longest-serving Bucs coach of all time. Jon Gruden coached the Buccaneers for 112 games, while Tony Dungy coached 96 games in Tampa Bay.

TONY DUNGY

Tony Dungy was hired to turn around the Buccaneers in 1996. That process began with the use of the cover 2 defense, which is now known as the Tampa 2, and widely copied throughout the NFL. Dungy is often credited with building the team that won Super Bowl XXXVII.

JON GRUDEN

Although he coached the Bucs for six seasons, Jon Gruden is most remembered for his first year there. In 2002, behind one of the greatest defenses in NFL history, the Bucs won a franchise-best 12 games. His Bucs captured their lone championship in Super Bowl XXVII.

LOVIE SMITH

Lovie Smith was hired by the Bucs to replace coach Greg Schiano just a week after the 2013 season ended. Smith had previously been the head coach of the Chicago Bears, taking them to the Super Bowl in 2006. Before that, Smith was a Buccaneer linebackers coach under Tony Dungy.

The Mascot

Captain Fear is huge, standing 6 feet, 2 inches tall and 250 pounds.

Bruce the Buccaneer was the original Bucs mascot when they opened play in 1976. The winking pirate with the big hoop earring and the knife in his mouth was also the logo featured on the Buccaneer helmets. When the bright orange color scheme gave way to the more conservative red, black and pewter in 1996, Bruce lost his place on the helmet and his role as team mascot.

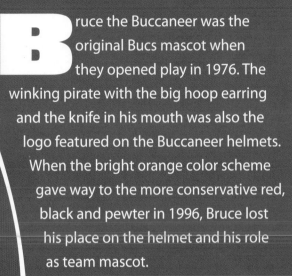

Captain Fear loves the song "Yo Ho, Yo Ho, A Pirate's Life for Me" and the movie *The Little Mermaid*.

The Bucs did not have a mascot over the next four seasons. Captain Fear, a feisty Caribbean pirate with blue eyes, black hair, thick eyebrows and a full beard, took over duties in 2000. He watches over the city of Tampa from the "crow's nest." This is a structure at the top of the pirate ship harbored at Buccaneer Cove.

Captain Fear claims Falcons, the ones from Atlanta, are his favorite meal.

Legends of the Past

Many great players have suited up in the Buccaneers' red and pewter. A few of them have become icons of the team and the city it represents.

Warren Sapp

Position Defensive Tackle
Seasons 13 (1995–2007)
Born December 19, 1972, in Orlando, Florida

Warren Sapp was the 12th pick in the 1995 **NFL Draft**. He earned seven trips to the Pro Bowl in nine seasons with the Bucs, was the Defensive Player of the Year in 1999, and was a key player on the 2002 Super Bowl team. Working in the Tampa 2 defense, Sapp was one of the most active defensive players in NFL history. He seemed to be involved in every play. His 96.5 career sacks are the second-highest total for any defensive tackle. In 2013, Sapp was voted into the hall of fame.

John Lynch

John Lynch played his college football at Stanford University and was picked by the Bucs in the third round of the 1993 draft. Lynch ended up being a nine-time Pro Bowler, earning the reputation as one of the hardest hitting safeties in NFL history. Although he earned his Super Bowl ring with the Bucs in 2002, Lynch had the respect of his peers well before that. He was recently listed as one of the "Top 10 Most Feared Tacklers" on an NFL Films production, an honor he shares with players like Lawrence Taylor, Dick Butkus, and Ronnie Lott.

Position Strong Safety
Seasons 15 (1993–2007)
Born September 25, 1971, in Hinsdale, Illinois

Derrick Brooks

Derrick Brooks was drafted by the Buccaneers in the first round in the 1995 NFL Draft. He went on to play his entire career for the Bucs. The 11-time Pro Bowl linebacker was named NFL Defensive Player of the Year in 2002, recording 117 tackles and a sack. The most amazing statistic of the 2002 season was that Brooks scored five defensive touchdowns, an NFL record for a linebacker. He is also one of six players in NFL history to make the Pro Bowl, be named Defensive Player of the Year, and win a Super Bowl in the same season.

Position Linebacker
Seasons 14 (1995–2008)
Born April 18, 1973, in Pensacola, Florida

Lee Roy Selmon

Lee Roy Selmon was the first player to call himself a Tampa Bay Buccaneer after being chosen with the first overall pick in the 1976 draft. During his first season, Selmon earned the team award for Rookie of the Year, and the team **Most Valuable Player (MVP)** award, rather easily. Selmon was often the lone bright spot during dark times for the Bucs. He represented the team in six straight Pro Bowls and was honored as the NFL Defensive Player of the Year in 1979. Unfortunately, Selmon had his career cut short by a back injury in 1984. The Bucs retired his number, 63, in 1986.

Position Defensive Lineman
Seasons 9 (1976–1984)
Born October 20, 1954, in Eufaula, Oklahoma

Stars of Today

Today's Buccaneers team is made up of many young, talented players who have proven that they are among the best players in the league.

Vincent Jackson

Vincent Jackson played for the San Diego Chargers for seven seasons, earning three trips to the Pro Bowl. Jackson landed on the Bucs in 2012 and impressed his new team right away. He finished with 72 catches for 1,384 yards. Jackson's total yards nearly passed Mark Carrier, who set the mark for single season receiving yards in 1989. In 2013, Jackson picked up where he left off by setting multiple Buccaneer records in an October game against the New Orleans Saints. He caught the longest reception in team history, at 95 yards, and recorded the most receiving yards in a single game, with 216 yards.

Position Wide Receiver
Seasons 9 (2005–2013)
Born January 14, 1983, in Colorado Springs, Colorado

Doug Martin

After a successful college career at Boise State University, Doug Martin won a starting job in 2012 with a breakout pre-season. The shifty running back never slowed down. Martin finished his rookie season with 1,454 rushing yards, breaking the single-season Bucs rookie rushing record set by Cadillac Williams. Martin also racked up close to 500 receiving yards. All in all, he pulled off one of the greatest offensive seasons in Buccaneer history.

Position Running Back
Seasons 2 (2012–2013)
Born January 13, 1989, in Oakland, California

Alterraun Verner

A brilliant high school athlete, Alterraun Verner used to tutor his teammates in math and history. After being selected by the Tennessee Titans in the 2010 NFL Draft, Verner returned to the University of California, Los Angeles (UCLA), in the 2011 offseason to finish his bachelor of science degree in mathematics. By 2013, this scholar had mastered the cornerback position. Verner improved steadily in each of his first three seasons with the Titans. In 2013, he led the team with five interceptions, 23 passes defended, and made the Pro Bowl. After that season, he signed a free-agent contract with the Bucs, replacing Darrelle Revis as the newest shutdown cornerback in Tampa Bay.

Position Cornerback
Seasons 4 (2010–2013)
Born December 13, 1988, in Orange, California

A fter his first training camp, former coach Greg Schiano had high praise for Lavonte David, describing him as an unselfish player who loves the game and is always prepared. The second round pick from Nebraska lived up to the high praise from his coach during his rookie season. In fact, he led the entire Bucs team with 139 tackles in 2012, while starting all 16 games at outside linebacker. David also posted 20 tackles-for-loss, the most by a rookie since Kendrell Bell of the Pittsburgh Steelers back in 2001.

Position Linebacker
Seasons 2 (2012–2013)
Born January 23, 1990, in Miami, Florida

All-Time Records

592 All Time Most Points

Bucs kicker Martin Gramatica booted through 181 **extra points** and 137 field goals during his five-year tenure, scoring more points than any other Buc in franchise history.

14,820 Career Passing Yards

In six seasons as the Bucs' quarterback, Vinny Testaverde threw for close to 15,000 yards and 77 touchdown passes.

58 All-time Rushing Touchdowns

Mike Alstott ran the ball with great power, often knocking two or three defenders over on a single run. The tough fullback ran for more than 5,000 yards as a Buccaneer on his way to setting the all-time Bucs mark for rushing touchdowns.

4,065
Single Season Passing Yards

In 2012, quarterback Josh Freeman became the first player in Bucs history to throw for 4,000 yards in a season. In 2012, 11 quarterbacks had more than 4,000 yards passing, an NFL record.

106 Single Season Receptions

Keyshawn Johnson caught 106 passes for 1,266 yards in his second season with the Buccaneers in 2001.

Timeline

Throughout the team's history, the Tampa Bay Buccaneers have had many memorable events that have become defining moments for the team and its fans.

1992

Under new coach Sam Wyche, the Bucs get off to a great start, winning three of their first four games. However, the Bucs then lose 10 of the next 11 games. At the end of the 1992 season, Vinny Testaverde is released.

1976

The expansion Buccaneers enter the league alongside the Seahawks. The Bucs play their first season in the AFC West, knowing that the following year they would move to the NFC Central Division. Under the direction of coach John McKay, they finish 0-14.

In 1998, Raymond James Stadium opens on September 20th to a sellout crowd of more than 67,000 fans.

| 1970 | 1975 | 1980 | 1985 | 1990 | 1995 |

1996

Tony Dungy takes over as head coach for the new-look Bucs. The team completely transforms its style, removing the orange colors and the Bucco Bruce pirate logo in favor of a tougher look, featuring red, black, pewter, and dark orange, as well as a menacing looking pirate flag.

1979

With a record of 9-7, the Bucs capture their first division title behind defensive lineman Lee Roy Selmon, who earns Defensive Player of the Year honors. The Bucs beat the Philadelphia Eagles in their first playoff game, 24-17, at Tampa Stadium.

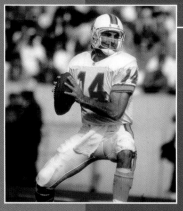

1987

The Bucs draft Vinny Testaverde in the first round. To make room on the roster for the young quarterback from the University of Miami, the Bucs famously trade Steve Young to the 49ers. Young would go on to become one of the greatest quarterbacks in NFL history.

2002

Tony Dungy is replaced by Jon Gruden. In his first season as Bucs coach, Gruden leads the team to a franchise best 12-4 record behind one of the greatest defenses in NFL history. Derrick Brooks is named Defensive Player of the Year, although the award could easily have been given to Warren Sapp, John Lynch, or the NFC sack leader, Buccaneer Simeon Rice. The Bucs cruise through the playoffs and defeat the Raiders in the Super Bowl.

In 2010, the Buccaneers take the field with the youngest roster in the NFL, finishing with a record of 10-6, but narrowly missing the playoffs.

The Future

With young studs Lavonte David, Mason Foster, and Dashon Goldson on the roster, the future in Tampa is bright. The task of winning a second Super Bowl falls on new Head Coach Lovie Smith. On the offensive side, Smith also has plenty of talent to work with. Speedy running back Bobby Rainey, who came on late in 2013, is a great compliment to the smooth running style of Doug Martin, who has established himself as one of the very best in the NFL.

| 2000 | 2003 | 2006 | 2009 | 2011 | 2014 |

In 2005, the Bucs win 11 games and capture their fifth division title.

2008

The Bucs end the season on a losing streak and decide to fire Gruden, the coach who brought them their only Super Bowl victory. Clearly beginning a rebuilding process behind new head coach Raheem Morris, the Bucs move on from veterans Derrick Brooks, Jeff Garcia, Ike Hilliard, Joey Galloway, Warrick Dunn, and Brian Griese.

2012

Coach Greg Schiano signs Eric LeGrand, a player paralyzed two years earlier at Rutgers to an inspirational honorary contract. He invites LeGrand to training camp where he becomes an inspirational figure for the Bucs.

Write a Biography

Life Story

A person's life story can be the subject of a book. This kind of book is called a biography. Biographies often describe the lives of people who have achieved great success. These people may be alive today, or they may have lived many years ago. Reading a biography can help you learn more about a great person.

Get the Facts

Use this book, and research in the library and on the Internet, to find out more about your favorite Buccaneer. Learn as much about this player as you can. What position does he play? What are his statistics in important categories? Has he set any records? Also, be sure to write down key events in the person's life. What was his childhood like? What has he accomplished off the field? Is there anything else that makes this person special or unusual?

Use the Concept Web

A concept web is a useful research tool. Read the questions in the concept web on the following page. Answer the questions in your notebook. Your answers will help you write a biography.

Concept Web

□

Adulthood
- Where does this individual currently reside?
- Does he or she have a family?

□

Your Opinion
- What did you learn from the books you read in your research?
- Would you suggest these books to others?
- Was anything missing from these books?

□

Childhood
- Where and when was this person born?
- Describe his or her parents, siblings, and friends.
- Did this person grow up in unusual circumstances?

□

Accomplishments off the Field
- What is this person's life's work?
- Has he or she received awards or recognition for accomplishments?
- How have this person's accomplishments served others?

Write a Biography

□

Help and Obstacles
- Did this individual have a positive attitude?
- Did he or she receive help from others?
- Did this person have a mentor?
- Did this person face any hardships?
- If so, how were the hardships overcome?

□

Accomplishments on the Field
- What records does this person hold?
- What key games and plays have defined his or her career?
- What are his or her stats in categories important to his or her position?

□

Work and Preparation
- What was this person's education?
- What was his or her work experience?
- How does this person work; what is the process he or she uses?

Trivia Time

Take this quiz to test your knowledge of the Tampa Bay Buccaneers.
The answers are printed upside-down under each question.

1 In what year did the Buccaneers begin play as an expansion team?

A. 1976

2 Which NFL team joined the league at the same time as the Bucs?

A. The Seattle Seahawks

3 What Buccaneer holds the team record for all-time rushing touchdowns?

A. Mike Alstott

4 Which Hall of Fame player did the Buccaneers trade away?

A. Steve Young

5 What was the name of the original Tampa Bay Buccaneers mascot?

A. Bruce the Buccaneer or Bucco Bruce

6 What is the name of the current Tampa Bay Buccaneers mascot?

A. Captain Fear

7 What are the Buccaneers' current colors?

A. Red, pewter, black, and a dash of orange

8 What sits harbored in Buccaneer Cove at Raymond James Stadium?

A. A 103-foot (31-meter) long replica pirate ship

9 Who was the head coach widely credited for building the defense that went on to capture Super Bowl XXXVII under Jon Gruden?

A. Tony Dungy

10 Who is the current head coach of the Buccaneers?

A. Lovie Smith

Key Words

.500: when a team wins and loses an equal number of games; in the NFL, an 8-8 record is a .500 season

alternate jersey: a jersey that sports teams may wear in games instead of their home or away uniforms

expansion teams: brand new teams in a sports league, usually from a city that has not hosted a team in that league before

extra points: attempts awarded after each touchdown scored that allows the offensive team to kick the ball through the goalposts for an extra point

hall of famer: a player judged to be outstanding in a sport

logo: a symbol that stands for a team or organization

merger: a combination of two things, especially companies, into one

Most Valuable Player (MVP): the player judged to be most valuable to his team's success

NFL Draft: an annual event where the NFL chooses college football players to be new team members

playoffs: the games played following the end of the regular season; six teams are qualified: the four winners of the different conferences, and the two best teams that did not finish first in their respective conference, called "wild cards"

Pro Bowler: an NFL player who takes part in the annual all-star game that pits the best players in the National Football Conference (NFC) against the best players in the American Football Conference (AFC)

sacks: when the quarterback, or another offensive player acting as a passer, is tackled behind the line of scrimmage before he can throw a forward pass

Super Bowl: the NFL's annual championship game between the winning team from the NFC and the winning team from the AFC

Index

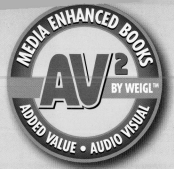

Log on to www.av2books.com

AV² by Weigl brings you media enhanced books that support active learning. Go to www.av2books.com, and enter the special code found on page 2 of this book. You will gain access to enriched and enhanced content that supplements and complements this book. Content includes video, audio, weblinks, quizzes, a slide show, and activities.

AV² Online Navigation

Book Pages
AV² pages directly correspond to pages in the book.

Audio
Listen to sections of the book read aloud.

Video
Watch informative video clips.

Key Words
Study vocabulary, and complete a matching word activity.

Embedded Weblinks
Gain additional information for research.

Quizzes
Test your knowledge.

Slide Show
View images and captions, and prepare a presentation.

Try This!
Complete activities and hands-on experiments.

AV² was built to bridge the gap between print and digital. We encourage you to tell us what you like and what you want to see in the future.

Sign up to be an AV² Ambassador at www.av2books.com/ambassador.

Due to the dynamic nature of the Internet, some of the URLs and activities provided as part of AV² by Weigl may have changed or ceased to exist. AV² by Weigl accepts no responsibility for any such changes. All media enhanced books are regularly monitored to update addresses and sites in a timely manner. Contact AV² by Weigl at 1-866-649-3445 or av2books@weigl.com with any questions, comments, or feedback.